THIS BOOK IS

. . . .

THE WORLD'S MOST HORRID/SEXY/
DISGUSTING /ATTRACTIVE/ BORING/
LOVABLE/UGLY/CUTE/ GEMINIAN.

YOURS IN DISGUST/ BEST WISHES
LOTS OF LOVE . . . .

P.S. PLEASE TAKE NOTE OF PAGE(S)

. . . .

THE GEMINI BOOK

A CORGI BOOK 0 552 12318 8

First publication in Great Britain
PRINTING HISTORY
Corgi edition published 1983
Corgi edition reissued 1984
Corgi edition reprinted 1985

Corgi Books are published by Transworld Publishers Ltd., Century House, 61-63 Uxbridge Road, Ealing, London W5 5SA, in Australia by Transworld Publishers (Aust.) Pty. Ltd., 26 Harley Crescent, Condell Park, NSW 2200, and in New Zealand by Transworld Publishers (N.Z.) Ltd., Cnr. Moselle and Waipareira Avenues, Henderson, Auckland.

Made and printed in Great Britain by the Guernsey Press Co. Ltd., Guernsey, Channel Islands.

THE GEMINI BOOK

BY IAN HEATH

GEMINI

MAY 21 — JUNE 20

THIRD SIGN OF THE ZODIAC
SYMBOL : THE TWINS
RULING PLANET : MERCURY
COLOURS : GREY, YELLOW
GEM : TOPAZ
NUMBER : FIVE
DAY : WEDNESDAY
METAL : QUICKSILVER, TIN
FLOWER : LILY OF THE VALLEY

.. LIKES DEALING WITH THE PUBLIC......

.... HAS PLENTY OF DRIVE..........

... JUGGLES WORDS WELL ....

.....HAS RED-HOT IDEAS.................

.... IS A TROUBLE-SHOOTER ....

..... A GOOD DELEGATOR ....

.... CANNOT SIT STILL ....

.......GETS ITCHY FEET..............

........DRESSES CONVENTIONALLY.......

... AND IS FAST-TALKING.

..... A SKI INSTRUCTOR..............

.....SCAFFOLDING ERECTOR..........

.... MATHEMATICIAN ....

.........LIFE-GUARD..............

..... A MEDICAL PERSON...........

..........ZOO-KEEPER................

... OR COMMERCIAL ARTIST.

The GEMINIAN at home...............

..... IS SECURITY MINDED.............

.... HAS A FULL LARDER ....

..... HATES GARDENING ....

.... LOVES GIVING PARTIES........

.... IS ALWAYS IN THE BATH...........

...... MAKES TASTY CAKES..........

... CAN'T MEND FUSES............

.....ENJOYS A LIE-IN..............

...... CAN BE MOODY....................

.... AND ARGUMENTATIVE.

The
GEMINIAN
likes.......................

......COOKING EXOTIC DISHES........

..... BEING SHOCKED..............

.......TROPICAL FISH................

. . . . GOLF. . . . .

.... BANANAS..................

.... AND CACTI.

.... LOSING............................

. . . . SPIDERS . . . .

..... GETTING FEET WET.............

.... TATTOOS ....

.... CUCKOO CLOCKS............

... AND FROGS-LEG SANDWICHES.

The
GEMINIAN
in love............

.... IS VERSATILE ....

.... CAN'T MAKE UP THEIR MINDS....

...... DOESN'T LIKE ROUTINE ....

..... FLIRTS OUTRAGEOUSLY.........

.............GIVING GIFTS.............

......ENJOYS NATURE WALKS........

.... BLUSHES EASILY............

......PURSUES RELENTLESSLY.......

... AND MAY HAVE SEVERAL LOVERS

GEMINIAN

AND PARTNER

HEART RATINGS

♥♥♥♥♥ WOWEE!!

♥♥♥♥ GREAT, BUT NOT 'IT'

♥♥♥ O.K. – COULD BE FUN

♥♥ FORGET IT

♥ WALK QUICKLY THE OTHER WAY

LIBRA   AQUARIUS

CANCER LEO ARIES TAURUS

VIRGO SAGITTARIUS
GEMINI

PISCES *SCORPIO*

CAPRICORN

GEMINI PEOPLE

QUEEN VICTORIA : BOB HOPE
ERROL FLYNN : PAUL GAUGUIN
ARTHUR CONAN DOYLE : AL JOLSON
THOMAS HARDY : VINCENT PRICE
JOHN FITZGERALD KENNEDY

DR JEKYLL AND MR HYDE
PAUL McCARTNEY : BURL IVES
PEGGY LEE : PAT BOONE
JUDY GARLAND : COLE PORTER
FRANK LLOYD WRIGHT : BOB DYLAN
PRINCE PHILIP : JANE RUSSELL
STAN LAUREL : BEATRICE LILLIE
DEAN MARTIN : IAN FLEMING
JOHN WAYNE : MARILYN MONROE
TONY CURTIS : JOHN DILLINGER
NANCY SINATRA : BASIL RATHBONE